Pathway to Grammar

Student's Book

2

Richmond

Richmond
58 St Aldates
Oxford
OX1 1ST
United Kingdom

Pathway to Grammar Student's Book Level 2

First Edition: 2015
Seventh Reprint: January 2023
ISBN: 978-607-06-1094-3

Av. Río Mixcoac No. 274, Col. Acacias,
Benito Juárez, C.P. 03240, Ciudad de México

Publisher: Justine Piekarowicz
Editorial Team: Jennifer S. Li, Joep van der Werff
Art and Design Coordinator: Marisela Pérez
Design: Erika Martínez
Layout: Paola Romero
Pre-Press Coordinator: Daniel Santillán
Pre-Press Team: Susana Alcántara, Virginia Arroyo
Cover Design: Erika Martínez

Cover Photograph: ©**THINKSTOCK:** iStock (ilona75, fcscafeine); Joep van der Werff; Polka Dot

Illustrations: Blanca Barrera pp. 15, 21, 35, 37, 56, 60, 76, 79; Laura González pp. 45, 46, 68, 70; Alejandro Herrerías p. 84, Diego Llanso pp. 7, 9, 27, 31, 49, 66, 69; Alma Nuñez pp. 17, 36, 43, 59, 77; Sara Palacios pp. 19, 38, 55, 58, 78; Emmanuel Urueta pp. 6, 10, 25, 28, 48, 65; Ismael Vázquez pp. 16, 39, 57, 75; David Yañez pp. 5, 8, 26, 29, 47, 50, 53, 67, 71

Photographs: ©**REPOSITORIO:** Ediciones Santillana, S.A. (Argentina) pp. 34, 40; Editorial Santillana, S.A. (Colombia) p. 83 (JHONNY FABIAN VILLARRAGA MARTÍNEZ); Editorial Santillana, S.A. (Guatemala) pp. 11, 23; Richmond Publishing S.A. de C.V. pp. 13 (Alejandro Herrerías), 23 (Marcela Gómez), 40 (Javier Montiel); Santillana de Ediciones, S.A. pp. 4, 11; Santillana del Pacífico, S.A. de Ediciones pp. 34, 36; Santillana Educación S.L. pp. 11 (COMSTOCK Photofile Limited), 13, 36 (FOTONONSTOP/INTERFOTONET DIFUSIÓN) 40 (HighRes Press Stock); ©**THINKSTOCK:** BananaStock pp. 48 (BananaStock), 79 (BananaStock); Blend Images pp. 20 (Shalom Ormsby), 58 (Jon Feingersh), 70 (Karin Dreyer); Creatas pp. 20 (Creatas Images), 54 (Jupiterimages), 58 (Creatas, Creatas Images, Jupiterimages), 74 (Jupiterimages), 77 (Creatas); Design Pics p. 7 (Design Pics); Digital Vision pp. 15 (Digital Vision), 44 (Digital Vision), 45 (Digital Vision), 57 (Martin Poole), 61 (Christopher Robbins), 61 (Michael Blann), 66 (Digital Vision), 77 (Ryan McVay); Dorling Kindersley RF pp. 14 (Howard Shooter), 73; Fuse pp. 4 (Fuse), 15 (Fuse), 20 (Fuse), 34 (Fuse), 36 (Fuse), 41 (Fuse), 46 (Fuse), 55 (Fuse), 61 (Fuse), 66 (Fuse), 69 (Fuse), 74 (Fuse), 79 (Fuse); Goodshoot p. 34 (Jupiterimages); Hemera pp. 4 (Dianne Maire, Vladimir Liverts, Oleg Saenko), 8 (Michael Kempf), 11 (Maxim Kazmin), 14 (Veronika Trofer), 19 (Dmitry Naumov), 25 (Tan Kian khoon), 26 (Ales Gavlovsky, Yuri Arcurs), 27 (Aidar Ayazbayev, Kristina Afanasyeva), 44 (Roman Sigaev), 54 (Rick Sargeant), 73, 74 (Elena Elisseeva, Anthony Douanne, Alena Yakusheva, Serghei Velusceac), 79 (Christophe Schmid, Artsiom Kireyau, Artsiom Kireyau); IndiaPicture p. 77 (Amit Somvanshi); iStock pp. 3-83 (Vladislav Ociacia), 4 (johnnyscriv, igor kisselev, fotostok_pdv, Sociologas, michaeljung, DarthArt, kuponjabah, anna1311, poligonchik), 6 (Anatoliy Samara), 7 (Glenda Powers, Tamara Kulikova, Jacek Chabraszewski, Kane Skennar), 8 (Stacey Newman, sezer66, IMNATURE, KatarzynaBialasiewicz, tellmemore000), 11 (SimonKr d.o.o., rep0rter, jeep5d, Aleosha, Oko_SwanOmurphy), 12 (Jorge Salcedo, XiXinXing, shironosov), 13 (alex_kz, Insanet, AlexandrMoroz), 14 (Vladimir Davydov, Jacek Chabraszewski, robinimages, poligonchik, Benjamin Simeneta, fotojagodka, AndreyPopov, peeravit18, saashi), 15 (IvonneW, ewastudio, VladMitrichev), 18 (digitalgenetics, miflippo), 19 (naumoid, alisbalb, trekandshoot, murengstockphoto, Kareivis, michaklootwijk, Alexandr Dubovitskiy, sunstock, desy_sevdanova), 20 (luismmolina, efesenko, _human), 22 (omgimages, pixelpot), 24 (Eric Isselée, Ameng Wu, PinkPueblo, szefei, nattanan726, michaeljung, eurobanks, thawats), 25 (Craig Dingle, vladimir kondrachov, warrengoldswain, nok6716, sylwia kania, vencavolrab), 26 (BartekSzewczyk, monkeybusinessimages, Tonis Valing, SergiyN), 27 (Eric Isselée, Bennewitz, Noam Kahalany, Jan Will, Myslitel, karandaev, gemenacom, daizuoxin), 29 (egal, fpdress, User63774ca5_63, Mandrixta, TuTheLens, Karpiyon), 30 (Eric Isselée, Alexia Khruscheva, Musat, spaxiax, kurkul, GlobalP, yongkiet, vencavolrab, Hung_Chung_Chih), 31 (Juanmonino), 32 (shironosov), 33 (Robert Churchill), 34 (Carl Kelliher, Steve Mcsweeny, GlenJ, DuÅ¡an KostiÄ, KatarzynaBialasiewicz, milllim, Tar_Heel_Rob), 35 (Jose Elias, Jitalia17, Matt Benoit, Sergey Peterman, Swetllana, GlobalP), 36 (cnrn, akova), 38 (Glenda Powers, Varina and Jay Patel, Thomas Perkins, Eric Isselée, PicturePartners, cookelma), 40 (dandanian, koosen, ShaunWilkinson, ISerg, trekandshoot, Vjom, extraded), 41 (Valeri Thoermer, mikanaka, lejoch), 44 (rzymu, Merih Unal Ozmen, GooDween123, zoom-zoom, PaulMichaelHughes, bloodua, Lusoimages, filmfoto, sam74100, joel-t, ValentynVolkov, margouillatphotos, Amawasri), 45 (Nicklas Karlsson, ariwasabi, Dario Lo Presti), 47 (Studio-Annika, Igor Mojzes, yaruta, brebca), 48 (GooDween123, Merih Unal Ozmen, rimglow, LUISMARTIN, Devonyu, anna1311, Goxi, ewastudio), 50 (Lusoimages, karammiri, goce risteski, vikif, akiyoko, Givaga), 51 (goce risteski, sonyae, oksun70, antares71), 52 (Jani Bryson, Roman_Gorielov, 4774344sean), 54 (Leslie Banks, Maria Pavlova, Jonas Gunnarsson, XiXinXing, Vacclav, ilona75, ValeriKimbro, AlinaMD, KatarzynaBialasiewicz, DragonImages, TKphotography64, MR1805), 55 (Anton Gvozdikov, david franklin, HoleInTheBucket, Jim Parkin, Artur Marciniec, Hoatzinexp, stuart renneberg), 58 (Josh Baker, g-stockstudio, TopPhotoImages), 61 (robertprzybysz), 62 (katkov, ValeriKimbro), 63 (fcscafeine), 64 (Leah-Anne Thompson, Eric Isselée, Glenda Powers, ClaudioVentrella, Buriy, gbh007, Magone, AndreyShtanko, VladislavMakarov, monkeybusinessimages, sserg_dibrova, zokru, chas53, LeventKonuk, Christian Musat), 66 (YanLev, mg7, monkeybusinessimages, fotokostic), 68 (james steidl, arlindo71, szefei, Teerapun, Eric Isselée, badmanproduction, Evgeny Kozhevnikov), 69 (Cliff Parnell, boguslavovna, Feverpitched), 72 (Leah-Anne Thompson, Peter Polák, Nicole S. Young), 73 (ewastudio, zokru, LeventKonuk, Grigoriy Lukyanov, Natikka, AlexStar, multik7, MikeyGen73), 74 (poligonchik, monkeybusinessimages, IPGGutenbergUKLtd, mycola, retrofutur, Natalia-flurno), 76 (_human, popovaphoto, Stanislav_K, pterwort, lucato), 77 (mvaligursky), 78 (gbh007, GlobalP, fotokostic, Yobro10), 79 (monkeybusinessimages, NADOFOTOS), 80 (Linda Yolanda), 81 (Rauluminate), 81, 82 (Jacek Chabraszewski), 84, 85, 87, 88 (LeventKonuk),90 (_human); Liquidlibrary pp. 47 (Liquidlibrary), 69 (Jupiterimages); MIXA p. 22 (MIXA next); Monkey Business pp. 42 (Monkey Business Images), 55 (Monkey Business Images), 77 (Monkey Business Images), 79 (Monkey Business Images); moodboard pp. 24 (moodboard), 61 (moodboard); Photodisc pp. 4 (Medioimages/Photodisc), 7 (James Woodson), 24 (Ryan McVay), 26 (Jack Hollingsworth), 36 (Digital Vision), 46 (Ulrik Tofte), 61 (Photodisc), 64 (Photodisc), 74 (Digital Vision), 81 (Photodisc); PhotoObjects.net pp. 11 (Hemera Technologies), 19 (Hemera Technologies), 73 (Hemera Technologies), 76 (Hemera Technologies); Pixland p. 69 (Jupiterimages); Polka Dot pp. 14 (Jupiterimages), 38 (Jupiterimages), 81 (Jupiterimages); Purestock pp. 32 (Purestock), 58 (Purestock); Ron Chapple Studios p. 40 (Ron Chapple Stock); Stockbyte. pp. 11 (Stockbyte), 14 (Thinkstock Images), 15 (Jupiterimages), 27 (Stockbyte), 34 (Comstock Images, Jupiterimages), 40 (Stockbyte), 45 (Comstock Images, George Doyle), 48 (George Doyle), 55 (Brand X Pictures), 72 (Stockbyte), 74 (Brand X Pictures, Buccina Studios), 77 (George Doyle), 81 (Thinkstock Images), 82 (Comstock); Top Photo Group pp 4 (Top Photo Corporation), 44 (Top Photo Corporation), 48 (Top Photo Corporation); Wavebreak Media pp. 14 (Wavebreakmedia Ltd), 18 (Wavebreakmedia Ltd), 20 (Wavebreakmedia Ltd), 34 (Wavebreakmedia Ltd), 36 (Wavebreakmedia Ltd), 42 (Wavebreakmedia Ltd), 64 (Wavebreakmedia Ltd), 79 (Wavebreakmedia Ltd), 84, 85; Zoonar pp. 11 (Zoonar RF), 38 (Zoonar RF)

Printed in Brazil by Forma Certa

Lote: 774581
Código: 292710943

Contents

Unit			Page
Unit 1	Grammar	Possessive Adjectives. Prepositions *in, on, under.* Questions with prepositions. The question word *Where...?*	4
	Let's talk!	*Where are the pears? They're under here.*	
	Song	At School	
Unit 2	Grammar	Prepositions *in front of, behind, next to, between. There are some..., There aren't any..., Are there any...?, How many...?*	14
	Let's talk!	*Tom, what would you like for a snack? I would like some grapes. I'm sorry there aren't any grapes.*	
	Song	What Is It?	
Unit 3	Grammar	Regular and irregular plural nouns. Demonstratives *this, that, these, those. Is that...?, Are those...?*	24
	Let's talk!	*I like frogs. Do you like frogs, too? Yes, I do. And I love mice!*	
	Song	We're Different	
Unit 4	Grammar	Possessive pronouns. Present continuous, affirmative, negative, and interrogative. *What are you doing?*	34
	Let's talk!	*What do you like to do? I like walking the dog.*	
	Song	What Time Is It?	
Unit 5	Grammar	Present continuous with adjectives. Present continuous, negative. Present continuous, interrogative. Countable and uncountable nouns. *Any, some, a little, a lot.*	44
	Let's talk!	*Would you like some cereal? Yes, please. I'd like a little cereal. And would you like an apple?*	
	Song	A Costume Party	
Unit 6	Grammar	*Can* for ability, affirmative, negative and interrogative. Commands, affirmative and negative.	54
	Let's talk!	*Let's make a robot. Find a box. Okay. What now?*	
	Song	Pets	
Unit 7	Grammar	*Like* with nouns and gerunds. *What do you like? Which...do you like?*	64
	Let's talk!	*Would you like to ride bikes? No, thanks.*	
	Song	I like food.	
Unit 8	Grammar	Simple present for routines. Telling time. Simple present with time. Simple present, interrogative. Simple present, *Who...?*	74
	Let's talk!	*What do you do in the morning? I make the bed. I eat breakfast.*	
	Song	Tell Me About Bears	
	Grammar Summary		84
	Audio script		92
	Vocabulary list		96

Unit 1

bag

bookstore

box

frog

mother father

orange (*n, adj*)

park

playground

store

street

truck

zoo

in (*prep*) on (*prep*) under (*prep*)

Possessive adjectives

1 Read, write, and number.

My	Your	His	Her	Our	Your	Their

1. My dog is small. Your dogs aren't small. They're big!
2. ______ store is big. ______ store is big, too.
3. Her snake is short. ______ snake isn't short. It's long!
4. ______ mother is happy. ______ mother is happy, too.
5. ______ father is sad. ______ father is sad, too.

Possessive adjectives, interrogative

1 Circle, look, and write.

1 

2 

3 

4 

5 

1. Is ***his*** / ***her*** / ***their*** T-shirt orange? Yes, it is ______________.
2. Is ***his*** / ***her*** / ***their*** ball pink? No, it isn't. It's ______________.
3. Are ***his*** / ***her*** / ***their*** balls small? ______________.
4. Is ***his*** / ***her*** / ***their*** T-shirt blue? ______________.
5. Are ***his*** / ***her*** / ***their*** socks purple? ______________.

Prepositions *in, on, under*

1 Decode and write.

Key
✕ = d
☺ = e
✎ = i
❍ = n
★ = o
■ = r
▼ = u

1 

✎ ❍

in

2 

▼ ❍ ✕ ☺ ■

____

3 

✎ ❍

____

4 

✎ ❍

____

5 

★ ❍

____

6 

✎ ❍

____

are
is

1. The cars *are in* ______ the street.
2. My mother ______________ the tree.
3. We ______________ the park.
4. The guitar ______________ the store.
5. They ______________ the playground.
6. The tiger ______________ the zoo.

Questions with prepositions 1

1 Look and write.

1. Is the sofa in the house? (*in the store*)

   No, it isn't. It's in the store ______.

2. Are the bikes on the truck? (*in the street*)

   No, they aren't. They're ______.

3. Is the dog on the chair? (*under the table*)

   ______.

4. Is the frog in the zoo? (*on my finger*)

   ______.

5. Are the oranges on the trees? (*on the truck*)

   ______.

6. Is the horse in the park? (*on the playground*)

   ______.

Where...?

1 Trace and write.

1. *Where are* ____ the books? *They're in* ____ the bookstore.
2. *Where* ____ the cat? *It's* ____ the chair.
3. ____ the dog? ____ the truck.
4. ____ the carrots? ____ the box.
5. ____ the chicken? ____ the truck.
6. ____ the flowers? ____ the table.

2 Look, read, and write.

1. Where are your red socks ?
2. my green shirt ?
3. ?
4. ?
5. ?
6. ?

3 Look again and answer.

1. They're on the yellow shirt .
2. It's under .
3. .
4. .
5. .
6. .

4 Read and match.

1. The small truck is under the chair. The big truck is in the street.
2. The tall bike is in the street, too. The short bike is in the park.
3. The happy teddy bear is in the bag, and the sad teddy bear is on the bookcase.

5 Write, color, and draw.

1. The *yellow flowers are* ____________ in the bag.
2. The blue ____________________ on the table.
3. The ____________________ under the table.

Let's talk!

1 Listen and write. 2

FATHER: *Where are* ________ the pears?

GRACE: ________ here.

Here ________ are.

FATHER: ________ you!

GRACE: Where's the ________?

FATHER: It's ________.

________ you are.

GRACE: ________!

2 Read the dialogue with a friend.

3 Talk with a friend. Then write.

A: Where ________?

B: ________ (*in* / *under*) here.

Here you are.

A: Thank you!

B: Where ________?

A: ________ (*in* / *under*) here.

Here you are.

A: Thank you!

Let's sing!

1 Listen and trace. 3

At School

Where is my orange pencil case?
It's in the schoolbag.

Where is my purple drum?
It's on the table.

Where is my yellow glue stick?
It's under the chair.

These are my scissors.
Who put them there?

2 Now, write and draw.

Where is my ________________?

It's __________ the __________.

Unit 2

rooms

duck

bathroom

bedroom

garden

kitchen

living room

dining room

mirror

radio

television, TV

toys

behind (*prep*)   in front of (*prep*)

between (*prep*)

next to (*prep*)

Prepositions *behind, in front of* 4

1 Look and write.

behind   in front of

1

2

3

4

5

6

1. The cat is *in front of* the mirror.
2. My brother is ____________ the bike.
3. My dad is ____________ the car.
4. The girl is ____________ the toys.
5. The garden is ____________ the house.
6. The picture is ____________ the boy.

1 Look and number.

1 bathroom 2 bedroom 3 dining room 4 kitchen 5 living room

2 Look again and circle.

1. Where is the living room?
   It's ***next to*** / ***between*** the dining room.
2. Where is the bathroom?
   It's ***next to*** / ***between*** the bedrooms.
3. The kitchen is ***next to*** / ***between*** the dining room.
4. The dining room is ***next to*** / ***between*** the living room and the kitchen.

There are some, There aren't any

1 Look, color, and mark (✓ or ✗).

✓	apples		chickens		houses		toys
	cats		ducks		stores		trees

2 Look again and write.

1. *There are some* ____ apples.
2. ____ *aren't any* cats.
3. ____ stores.
4. ____ toys.
5. ____ ducks.
6. ____ houses.
7. ____ trees.
8. ____ chickens.

1 Look, count, and write.

1. Are there any rooms?
   Yes, there are.
   There are four rooms.
2. Are there any bathrooms?
   No, ________________
   ____
3. Are there any bedrooms?
   ____
   ____
4. Are there any chairs?
   ____
   ____
5. Are there any beds?
   ____
   ____
6. Are there any mirrors?
   ____
   ____

How many...?

1 Find, count, and write.

1. *How many* snakes *are there* ______? *There are three snakes* ______.
2. ______ kites *are there* ______? *There aren't any kites* ______.
3. ______ TVs ______? ______.
4. ______ ducks ______? ______.
5. ______ radios ______? ______.
6. ______ robots ______? ______.
7. ______ pencils ______? ______.
8. ______ apples ______? ______.

2 Look, listen, and write. 5

1. How many beds *are in the kitchen* ?

   There aren't any beds in the kitchen .

2. How many cats ______________________________ ?

   ______________________________ .

3. How many people ______________________________ ?

   ______________________________ .

4. How many colors ______________________________ ?

   ______________________________ .

5. How many Harlem Globetrotters ______________________________ ?

   ______________________________ .

3 Draw and write.

How many ___________ are on your TV program?

____

4 Look and write.

CHARLIE:	MR. SMITH:
1. Do you *have any* pencils?	2. No, *I don't have any pencils*.
3. Do you *have an* eraser?	4. No, ______.
5. Do you ______ books?	6. ______.
	7. I ______ balls.
	8. I ______ bikes.
9. Do you ______ radios?	10. ______!

5 Draw and write.

Rooms in My House

1. How many bedrooms do you have? ______
2. How many bathrooms are there? ______

1 **Listen and write.** 6

MOM: Tom, what would you like for a snack?

TOM: I would like *some grapes*.

MOM: I'm sorry! There ____________________. But there are ______________. Would you like ____________?

TOM: No, thank you. I'd like ____________.

MOM: ______________.

TOM: ____________!

2 **Read the dialogue with a friend.**

3 **Talk with a friend. Then write.**

A: Would you like some __________?

B: No, thank you.

I would like some __________ .

A: There aren't any __________.

But there are some __________.

B: Great. I'd like some __________, please.

A: __________. Here you are.

B: Thank you!

Let's sing!

1 Listen and color. 7

What Is It?

Stand up, listen, sing and look.
What is it?
It's a red book.

Sit down, come, see and stop.
What is it?
It's a brown dog.

How many bluebirds?
One and two.

How many school friends? Me and you.

B

Unit 3

C

alphabet

letter

A

animals

bird

crocodile

lizard

monkey

body

head

tail

legs

hair

face

1 child, 2 children

1 man, 2 men

1 woman, 2 women

Plural nouns, regular

1 **Look and mark *S* (singular) or *P* (plural).**

1  P

2 

3 

4 

5 

6 

2 **Look again and write.**

bird car elephant giraffe lizard tree

1. Where *are* the *birds*? *They're here*.
2. Where *is* the ______? *It's there*.
3. Where ______ the ______? ______.
4. Where ______ the ______? ______.
5. Where ______ the ______? ______.
6. Where ______ the ______? ______.

Plural nouns, irregular

1 Complete and solve.

Across →

2 (*foot*) His ___*feet*___ are on the table.

3 (*man*) The __________ are under the car.

4 (*child*) The __________ are on the playground.

Down ↓

1 (*woman*) The __________ are in front of the house.

2 (*fish*) The __________ are in the water.

3 (*mouse*) The __________ are in the garden.

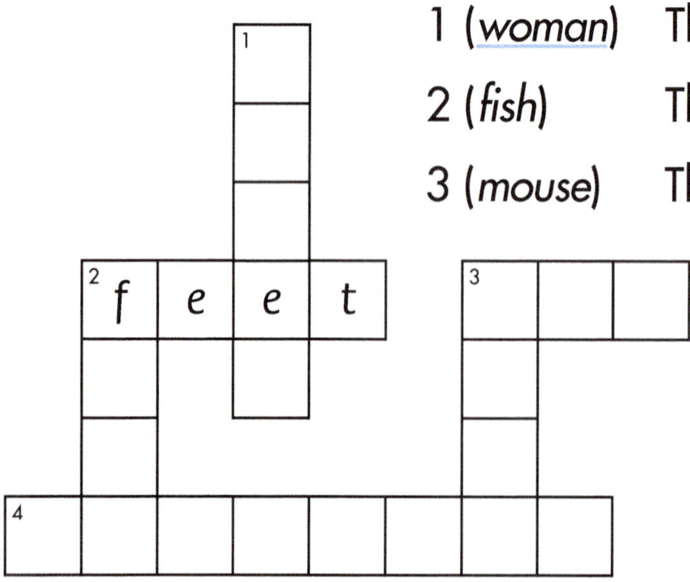

Demonstratives *this, that*

1 Look and sort.

apple bike crocodile guitar monkey pen phone tree

Here: *phone,* ____________________

There: *apple,* ____________________

2 Read, look again, and write.

1. *This is* a pen.
2. *That is* a bike.
3. ________ a monkey.
4. ________ a phone.
5. ________ a crocodile.
6. ________ a tree.
7. ________ a guitar.
8. ________ an apple.

Demonstratives *these, those*

1 Look and color.

★ = orange	■ = red	◗ = blue	▲ = green	● = brown	✦ = yellow

2 Read, look, and write.

TEACHER: *These aren't* green apples. *These are yellow apples*.

TEACHER: *Those aren't* red toys. *Those* ______________.

GIRL: ______________ yellow books. ______________.

GIRL: ______________ brown animals. ______________.

TEACHER: ______________ orange letters. ______________.

GIRL: ______________ purple teddy bears. ______________.

Practice with the Pathway to Certification app!

Is that...? Are those...? 8

1 Look and write.

1 

Is that an elephant?

Yes, that is an elephant.

2 

Are these monkeys?

No, these aren't monkeys. They *are cats*.

3 

__________ mice?

__________.

4 

__________ lizard?

__________. It's __________.

5 

__________ monkeys?

__________. They __________.

6 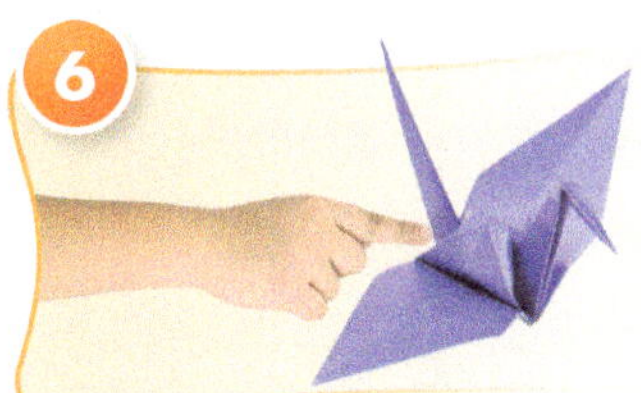

__________ bird?

__________.

2 Look, read, and write.

1  Is this my tail?  No, that isn't your tail .

2  Is this its body?  ________________________
________________________.

3  Is this his hair?  ________________________
________________________.

4  Are these our legs? 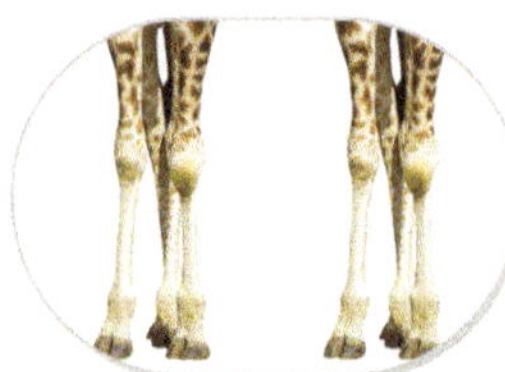 ________________________
________________________.

5  Are these their faces?  ________________________
________________________.

3 Read, circle, and draw.

This / ***These*** animal has a tail.

That / ***Those*** animals have four legs.

4 Find, color, and write.

1. What's this ______________?
   This is the letter P ______________.

2. What's that ______________?
   That ______________.

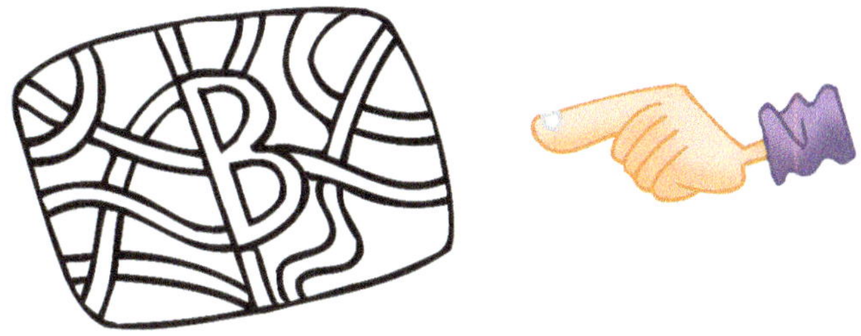

3. ______________?
   ______________.

4. ______________?
   ______________.

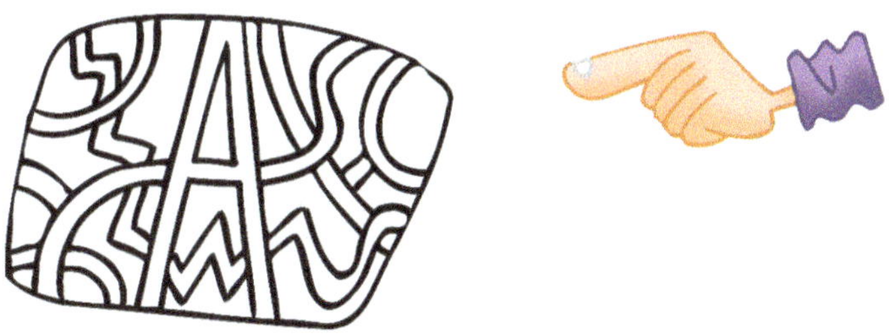

5. ______________?
   ______________.

6. ______________?
   ______________.

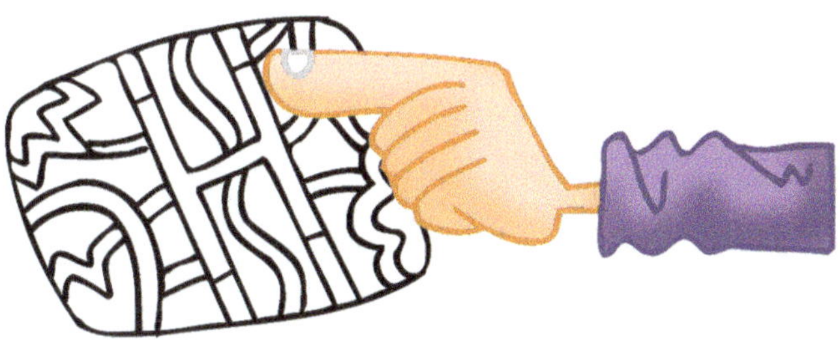

5 Look again, decode, and write.

What's this?

This is the ___ ___ ___ ___ ___ ___ ___ T .
3 4 1 5 3 2 6

1 Listen and write. 9

ALEX: I like ___frogs___. Do you like ________, too?

BILL: ____________. And I love ________!

SUE: Me, too! Do you like ________?

BILL: ____________!

ALEX: So do I!

2 Read the dialogue with two friends.

3 Talk with two friends. Then write.

A: I like ____________. Do you like ____________, too?

B: Yes / No, I ____________. And / But I love ____________.

C: Me, too! Do you like ____________?

B: I like / love ____________.

A: So do I!

Let's sing!

1 Listen and write. 10

He His She Her We

We're Different

_____ has brown eyes,
_____ hair is blond.
_____ has green eyes,
_____ legs are long.

_____ has black hair,
And _____'s short.
_____'re great friends,
I like them all.

_____'re different,
_____'re not the same.
_____ all like to play this game.

_____'re different,
_____'re not the same.
_____ all like to play this game!

2 Now write. Compare yourself with a friend.

_____ has _________ _________. My _____ is _________.

_____ has _________ _________. My _____ are _________.

We are different!

Unit 4

baseball

basketball

bounce (v)

camera

clean (v)

door

close (v)

open (v)

fish (v)

hit (v)

kick (v)

paint (v)

play tennis, baseball (v)

walk (v)

watch (v)

Possessive pronouns

1 Read and match. Use colors.

1. my shirt			theirs
2. their door			ours
3. her socks			mine
4. his camera			hers
5. our baseball			yours
6. your fish			his

2 Look, compare, and write.

1. Is this mine?
*No, it's ours*______.

2. Are these hers?
__________________.

3. Are these ours?
__________________.

4. Is this theirs?
__________________.

5. Is this his?
__________________.

6. Is this yours?
__________________.

1 Look and unscramble.

1. ylpa nnesti *play tennis*
2. ihfs ____________
3. thwac ____________
4. cobeun ____________

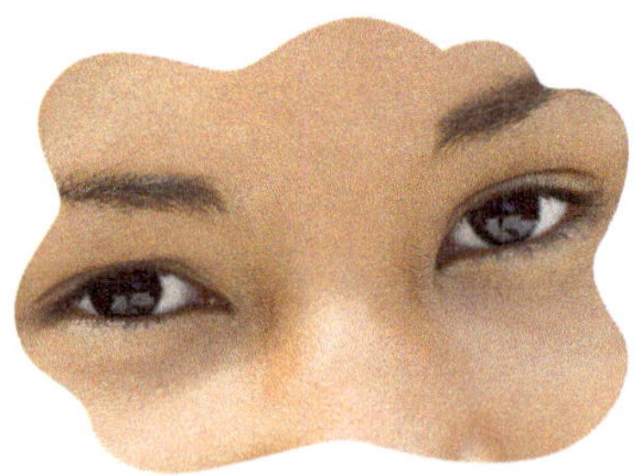

2 Look again and write. Then number.

1. Vicky and her mother *are playing tennis*.
2. I ____________ in the sea.
3. Grandpa ____________ TV.
4. We ____________ a ball.

Practice with the Pathway to Certification app!

Present continuous, negative

1 Number.

1 eating
2 taking a picture
3 jumping
4 throwing
5 playing
6 watching

2 Read, look, and write.

1. Rick __*isn't*__ jumping. *He's eating* ________ a sausage.
2. Tammy ________ playing baseball. *She's* ________.
3. Kim ________ taking a picture. ________.
4. Tom ________ eating. ________ the ball.
5. They ________ watching the game. ________ baseball.
6. Tom's mom and dad ________ throwing the ball. ________.

Present continuous, interrogative

1 Read, look, and write.

1 
2 
3 
4 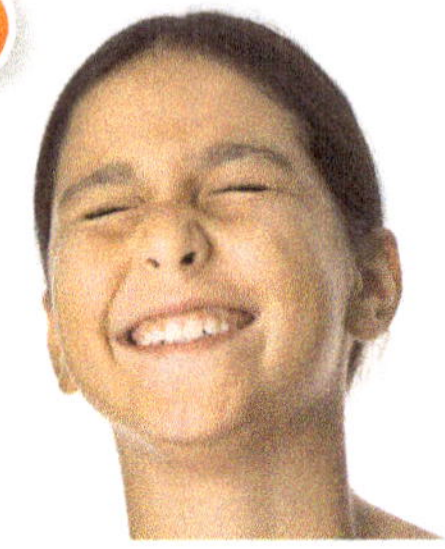
5 
6 
7 
8 

1. (*catch*) __Is__ Ben __catching__ the apples? __Yes__, he __is__.
2. (*play*) ______ we __________ the piano? _____, you ______.
3. (*kick*) ______ the horse __________? ________________.
4. (*open*) ______ she __________ her eyes? ________________.
5. (*paint*) ______ Grace __________ her hand? ________________.
6. (*clean*) ______ I __________? ________________.
7. (*walk*) ______ Dan __________ the dog? ________________.
8. (*swim*) ______ the fish __________? ________________.

What are you doing?

1 Trace and write.

close
hit
open
play

1 

2 

1. ____closing____ 2. ____________

3 

4 

3. ____________ 4. ____________

2 Look again and write.

1. What is Dad ____doing____? He's closing the door.
2. ________ the children ________? ________________.
3. ________ Grandma ________? ________________.
4. ________ your brothers ________? ________________.

3 Listen and mark (*T*, *L*, or *TL*). 12

T = Tony   L = Lucy   TL = Tony and Lucy

4 Read, look again, and write.

her   hers   his   their   theirs

1. *His* baseball is white.
2. The short robot is ______.
3. The purple basketball is ______.
4. ______ TV is big.
5. The small helicopter is ______.
6. ______ radio is yellow.
7. The orange cat is ______.
8. ______ camera is black.
9. The yellow clock is ______.
10. The blue bikes are ______.

5 Read, look, and write.

1 *paint / park*

Where are they *painting*?

They're painting in the park.

2 *kick the ball / kitchen*

__________ he __________?

He's __________ in the __________.

3 *fish / bathroom*

__________ she __________?

__________ in the __________.

4 *sleep / garden*

__________ the cat __________?

______________________________.

6 Read, write, and draw.

What are you doing?

I'm __________

in __________.

1 Listen and write. 13

Grace: What do you like to do?

Tom: I like walking the dog ________.

Grace: So do I. Do you like ________?

Tom: ________. ________ is fun!

Grace: Do you like ________?

Tom: ________!

Grace: I ________, either!

2 Read the dialogue with a friend.

3 Talk with a friend. Then write.

painting pictures | playing baseball | playing the piano | reading books

singing | swimming | writing | watching TV

A: What do you like to do?

B: I like ________.

A: So do I. Do you like ________?

B: Yes, I do. ________ is fun!

A: Do you like ________?

B: Yes, I do. / No, I don't.

A: So do I! / I don't, either!

Let's sing!

1 Listen and match. 14

What Time Is It?

6:00	8:00	9:00

Raymond Hannah Calvin

Unit 5

food

cake

chocolate

fish

fruit

juice

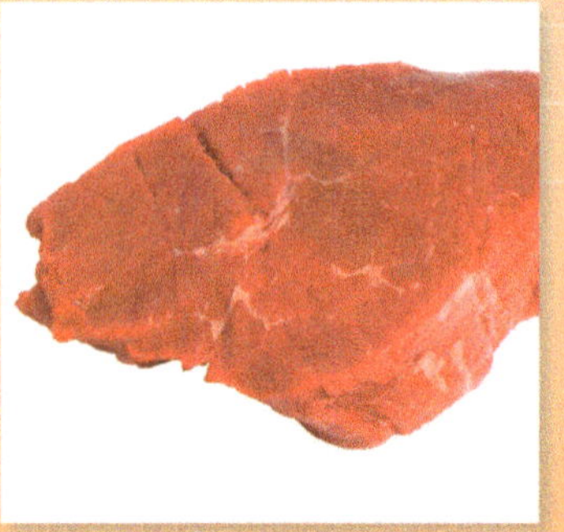

meat

rice

watermelon

beautiful (*adj*) ugly (*adj*)

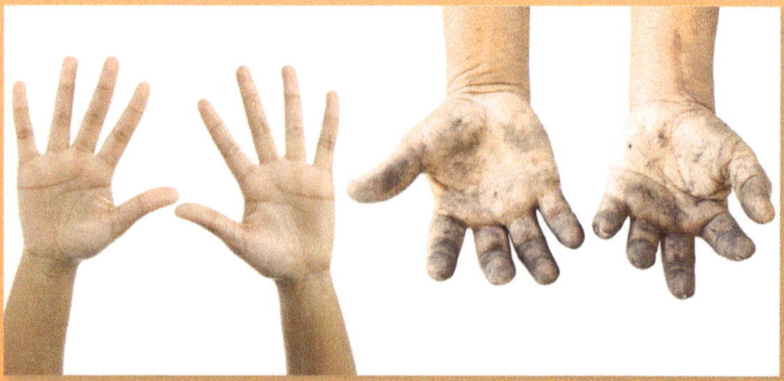

clean (*adj*) dirty (*adj*)

jacket

jeans

new (*adj*) old (*adj*)

Present continuous with adjectives

1 Look and circle.

1 

clean / *dirty* shirts

2 

new / *old* jeans

3 

big / *small* hats

4 

a *new* / *old* dress

5 

beautiful / *ugly* glasses

6 

clean / *dirty* shoes

2 Look again and write.

1. (*they*) They're wearing clean shirts__________.
2. (*you*) ______________________________.
3 (*we*) ______________________________.
4. (*she*) ______________________________.
5. (*he*) ______________________________.
6. (*I*) ______________________________.

F

Going to Work

My mom and dad **aren't wearing a gray jacket**. Dad **isn't wearing new shoes**.

1 Read and color.

▲ = black
○ = gray
● = pink
✧ = red
✖ = blue
✶ = green
◈ = purple
◖ = yellow

2 Look and write.

1. Tony _isn't wearing_ a pink shirt. _He's wearing a yellow shirt_.
2. Bill ____________ a yellow hat. ____________________________.
3. The teacher ____________ a blue skirt. ____________________________.
4. I ____________ a purple dress. ____________________________.
5. We ____________ green jackets. ____________________________.
6. Tom and Sue ____________ black jeans. ____________________________.

Present continuous, interrogative 15

1 Unscramble, look, and answer.

1. eating / a / big / you / watermelon / Are

   Are you eating a big watermelon ?

   Yes, we are .

2. Is / shoes / wearing / he / new

   ______________________________ ?

   ______________ .

3. photo / ugly / Are / an / taking / they

   ______________________________ ?

   ______________ .

4. beautiful / you / painting / a / picture / Are

   ______________________________ ?

   ______________ .

5. we / Are / an / car / cleaning / old / ?

   ______________________________ ?

   ______________ .

Countable and uncountable nouns

1 Find and sort.

Across:

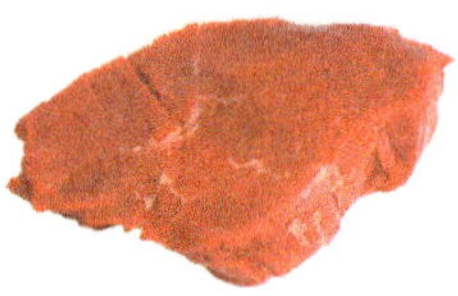

k	i	z	o	r	a	n	g	e	x	o
c	c	n	w	h	b	a	n	a	n	a
a	e	y	t	g	o	p	u	t	f	j
r	c	m	e	a	t	p	b	z	a	u
r	r	o	t	i	j	l	l	v	k	i
o	e	f	i	s	h	e	y	d	t	c
t	a	q	v	t	o	m	a	t	o	e
e	m	c	h	o	c	o	l	a	t	e

Down:

a / an...

orange

____

____

____

____

some...

ice cream

____

____

____

____

Uncountable nouns, *any*, *some*

1 Find, color, and write.

1. *There are some* bananas.
2. *There isn't any* bread.
3. ________________ ice cream.
4. ________________ watermelon.
5. ________________ water.
6. ________________ milk.
7. ________________ cake.
8. ________________ rice.
9. ________________ meat.
10. ________________ juice.

Uncountable nouns, *a little, a lot*

1 **Look and match.**

2 **Look again, read, and write.**

1. Is there any meat? *Yes, there's a little meat*_____.
2. Is there any rice? *Yes, there's* _______________.
3. Is there any milk? __________________________.
4. Is there any juice? __________________________.
5. Is there any cake? __________________________.
6. Is there any bread? __________________________.

3 Read, circle, and label.

1. Anna has **some** / **a** milk. She has **some** / **an** apple.
   She isn't eating her bread. She isn't wearing a hat.
2. Jake doesn't have **any** / **a** hat. He has a beautiful dog.
   Jake is eating **some** / **a** watermelon.
3. Lucy isn't eating watermelon. She is eating **some** / **a** bread.
   She has **some** / **a** grapes. She is wearing a yellow shirt.
4. Tom is wearing a yellow shirt, too. He doesn't have **any** / **a** food,
   but he has **some** / **a** water.

Lucy ______ ______ ______ ______

4 Write, circle, and draw.

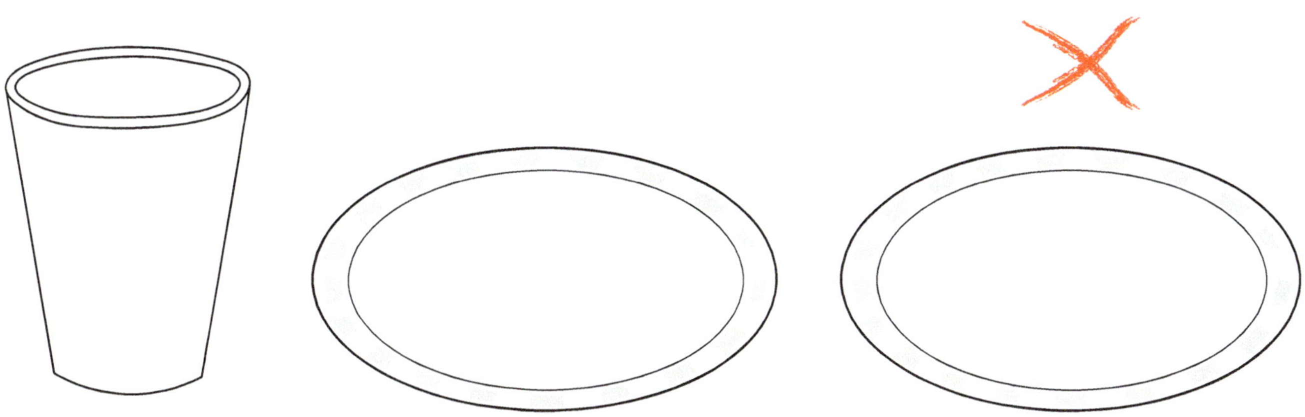

I have some ________. I have ***a*** / ***an*** ________.

I don't have any ________.

1 Listen and write. 16

DAD: Would you like ___some___ cereal?

SARA: Yes, please. I'd like __________ cereal.

DAD: And would you like __________?

SARA: Yes, please, I'd like one.

DAD: Would you like __________?

SARA: No, thank you. But I'd like __________.

2 Read the dialogue with a friend.

3 Talk with a friend. Then write.

A: Would you like some __________?

B: Yes, please. I'd like some / a little / a lot of __________.

A: Would you like a(n) __________?

B: Yes, please. I'd like one. / No, thank you.

But I'd like a(n) __________.

A: Here you are.

B: Thank you!

Let's sing!

1 Look, listen, and color. 17

A Costume Party

Costume Party!

Chorus:
It's hot and it's sunny;
We're in the park.
It's a great party.
We're all wearing hats.

Pete's wearing pink pants
And new shoes, too.
John's playing the recorder;
His T-shirt is blue.

Mike's wearing boots
And a long, blue coat.
Tam's wearing a dress
And she's drinking juice.

And look at Midge;
She has orange hair.
She's playing basketball
Dressed like a witch!

Costume party!

Unit 6

sea | beach | sand

boat

cut (v)

drive (v)

give (v)

make (v)

motorcycle

pick up (v)

bus

floor

plane

shell

spell (v)

sun

Can for ability, affirmative

1 Look and write.

cut
draw
drive
fly
make
pick up

1 

2 

3 

4 

5 

6 

1. He *can fly* a plane.
2. You __________ a sun.
3. She __________ a bus.
4. We __________ a cake.
5. I __________ a flower.
6. The truck __________ the box.

2 Write about yourself and draw yourself.

I can __________________.

1 Color. Then, mark (✗) the mistakes.

can't = ✗

2 Look again, read, and write.

1. *swim*: Motorcycles can't swim.
2. *use*: You ____________ a boat on the street.
3. *fly*: Grandma ______________.
4. *spell*: Mice ______________.
5. *eat*: The sun ______________ ice cream.

Can for ability, interrogative

1 Write, look, and match.

1. Can fish sit on the sand?
2. _____ dogs throw?
3. _____ shells play soccer?
4. _____ horses drive cars?
5. _____ cats spell?

- No, they can't, but they can swim in the sea.
- No, __________, but __________ catch the ball.
- __________, but __________ sit on the beach.
- __________, but __________ ride in trucks.
- __________, but __________ play with toys.

Commands, affirmative

1 Follow and write.

the baseball   your name   a book   your feet

some juice   some words   your hat   the big shell

1. *Find a book* in the bookcase.
2. ____________________!
3. ____________________ on the board.
4. ____________________ in the book.
5. ____________________!
6. ____________________!
7. ____________________, please.
8. ____________________ on the floor.

Commands, negative

1 Look, read, and write.

1. 

Don't put your shoes on the table! (*put*)

2. 

__________ the dog a sausage! (*give*)

3. 

__________ sand in the bed! (*put*)

4. 

__________ motorcycles in the house! (*ride*)

5. 

__________ in the living room! (*play tennis*)

6. 

__________ your hair! (*cut*)

7. 

__________ the floor! (*paint*)

8. 

__________ your dad's shoes! (*wear*)

2 Look, listen, and write the number. 19

3 Look again, read, and write.

1. How many watermelons can ______ Sam pick up?
   He can pick up three ______ watermelons.
2. How many ______ Ann and Grace walk?
   ______ dogs.
3. ______ Mr. Bill see in the bus?
   ______ children.
4. ______ the monkeys eat?
   ______ bananas.
5. ______ Jill take?
   ______ photos.
6. ______ Mom make?
   ______ cake.

4 Look and write. Then, answer for yourself.

can can't

fly play sail sing

1

Can you sail a small boat?

No, I can't.

2

_____ you _____ with sand on the beach?

_____, I _____.

3

_____ your father _____ a plane?

_____, _____.

4

_____ your friend _____ a song in English?

_____, _____.

5

Can you do this?

_____, I _____.

6

Can you do this?

_____, I _____.

Let's talk!

1 Listen and write. 20

cut	draw	find	make	put

PAT: Let's ___make___ a robot.

_________ a box.

NICK: Okay. What now?

PAT: _________ some circles for eyes.

_________ a mouth.

NICK: Okay. What's next?

PAT: _________ the box on your head.

NICK: Look! I'm a robot!

2 Read the dialogue with a friend.

3 Talk with a friend. Then write.

cut	go	look	make	paint	put

A: Now let's _________ a house! _________ a big box on the floor.

B: Okay. What now?

A: _________ a window. _________ the house.

B: Okay. What's next?

A: _________ in the house and _________ out!

B: Hello! You have a beautiful house!

Let's sing!

1 Listen and write. 21

fly jump run swim

happy sad sun

Pets

Rabbits can ________.

Cats can ________.

Spiders* can climb

Up to the ________!

Chorus:

They're good,

They're bad,

They're ________,

They're ________!

Fish can ________.

Dogs can ________.

Parrots can ________

Up to the sun!

*spider: see page 64.

2 Draw and write.

My Favorite Animal

This is a(n) ________________.

It can ________________________.

Unit 7

food

burger, hamburger

egg

fries, french fries

lemon

lemonade

mango

onion

peas

baby

family

old (*adj*) young (*adj*)

animals spider

1 hobby, 2 hobbies

sports

Like + noun, affirmative

1 Find, color, and write.

1 

Grandma *likes babies* ____________.

2 

I *like* __________________.

3 

She __________________.

4 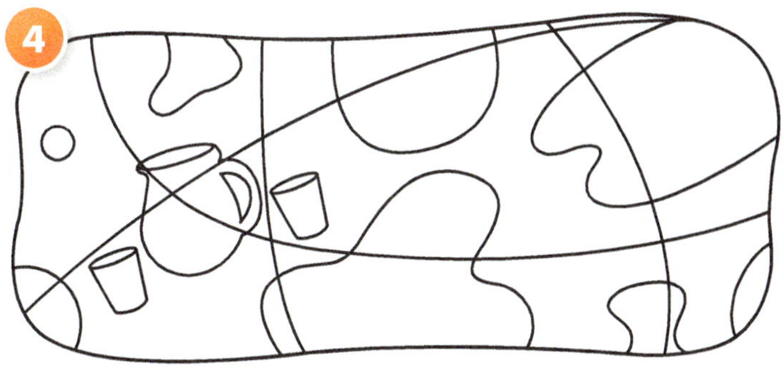

Jill and May __________________

5 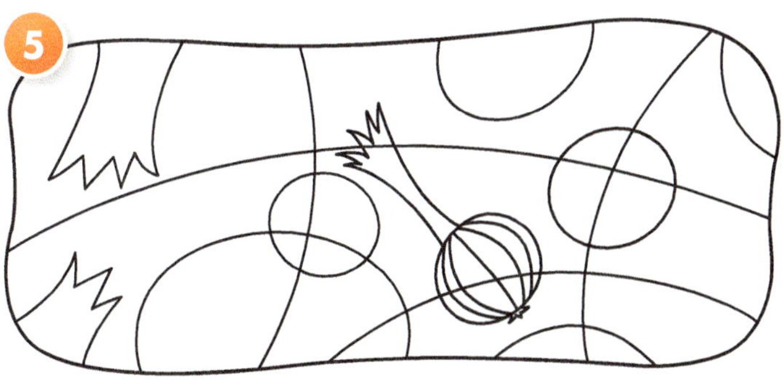

Dad __________________.

6 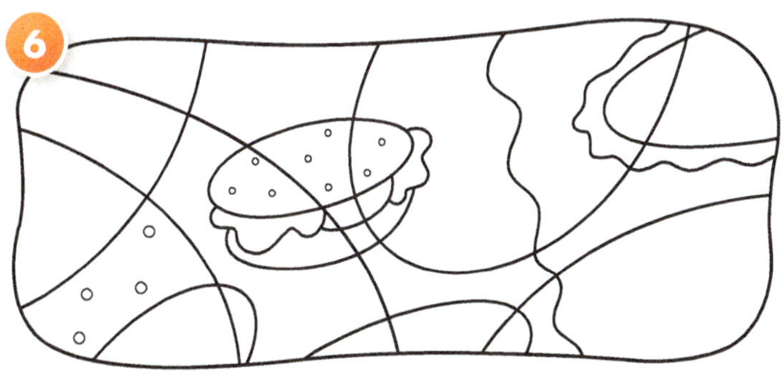

My dog __________________.

Like + gerund, affirmative

1 Look and write.

like	likes

fish	make	play	read	ride

1 

My family *likes reading* ____________.

2 

We ________________ the guitar.

3 

Elsa ________________ lemonade.

4 

You ________________ bikes.

5 

Grandpa ________________.

6 

They ________________ soccer.

Like, negative

1 Trace, look, and write.

clown
eggs
mango
onions
peas
spider

1. Grandma *doesn't like peas* ______.
2. I *don't* ______.
3. The baby ______.
4. The dog ______.
5. You ______.
6. They ______.

2 Write about yourself.

I like ______. I don't like ______.

Like, interrogative

1 Write and circle.

does doesn't

1. Does Mom like young cats?
   No, *she doesn't*.

2. ________ you like big burgers?
   Yes, *I do*.

3. ________ Nick like green spiders?
   No, ________.

4. ________ Tom and Kim like ugly dogs?
   Yes, ________.

5. ________ my father like old cars?
   Yes, ________.

6. ________ Anna like sad babies?
   No, ________.

Practice with the Pathway to Certification app!

What do you like? 22

1 Match and write.

do does

1.  my sister
2.  Alex and Lucy
3.  Ben
4.  Grandma
5.  they
6.  Mom

__________________________?
They like eggs.

__________________________?
She likes beautiful horses.

What does my sister like ?
She likes yellow pears.

__________________________?
He likes motorcycles.

__________________________?
She likes hats.

__________________________?
They like fries.

Which sport do you like?

1 Sort and draw.

Grandpa

Grace

2 Look again, read, and write.

1. *Which food* ______ does Grandpa like? He likes peas.
2. *Which animals does* Grandpa *like*? He likes tigers and lizards.
3. ____________ Grandpa ______? He likes playing the piano.
4. ____________ Grace ______? She likes mangoes.
5. ____________ Grace ______? She likes painting.
6. ____________ Grace ______? She likes basketball and tennis.

3 Answer for yourself and draw.

1. Which animals do you like?

   I like ______________________.

2. Which hobbies do you like?

   ______________________.

4 Look, read, and write.

her	my	their	your

JILL: Do you like _my_ new bike?

SUSY: Yes, I like _____ bike a lot!

MARK: I don't like _____ bike at all.

BILL: No, but I really like _____ bikes!

1 Listen and write 23

NICK: Would you like *to ride* ________ bikes?

PAT: No, ________. I don't like ________ bikes.

I like ________.

NICK: Sorry, I don't like ________.

PAT: Would you like ________ soccer?

NICK: Yes! Do you have ________?

PAT: ________.

2 Read the dialogue with a friend.

3 Talk with a friend. Then write.

A: Would you like to ________?

B: No, thanks. I don't like ________. I like ________.

A: Sorry, I don't like ________.

B: Would you like to ________?

A: Yes!

ride / riding (bikes, horses)
play / playing (soccer, the guitar)
paint / painting
sing / singing
draw / drawing
take / taking pictures

Let's sing!

1 Listen and mark (✓) or (✗). 24

✓

I Like Food

I like lemonade – I do.
I like tomatoes – and you?
I don't like carrots – no way!
I don't like hamburgers any day.

I like milk, and grapes, and bread.
I like chocolate bars and eggs.
I don't like potato chips – do you?
I like watermelon – I do.

✗

Unit 8

morning

afternoon

evening

night

breakfast

lunch

dinner

sleep (v)

bath

take a bath (v)

bed

make the bed (v)

go to school, to the park (v)

go home (v)

go to bed,
to sleep (v)

Simple present for routines

1 Unscramble.

1 

2 

3 

4 

gimrnon	ooferntan	ivgnene	gitnh
morning	______	______	______

2 Look again and write.

eat breakfast | go to bed | play basketball | take a bath

1. In the ______, *I eat breakfast*.
2. In the ______, ______.
3. In the ______, ______.
4. At night, ______.

1 Follow and write.

What time is it?

1:00 4:00 5:00 7:00 10:00 12:00

1. It's five o'clock.
2. It's ______.
3. It's ______.
4. ______.
5. ______.
6. ______.

2 Read, write, and circle.

1. What time is it? It's nine o'clock.
2. What ______? It's eight o'clock.
3. ______? It's eleven o'clock.

Simple present with time

1 Look and write.

doesn't
don't

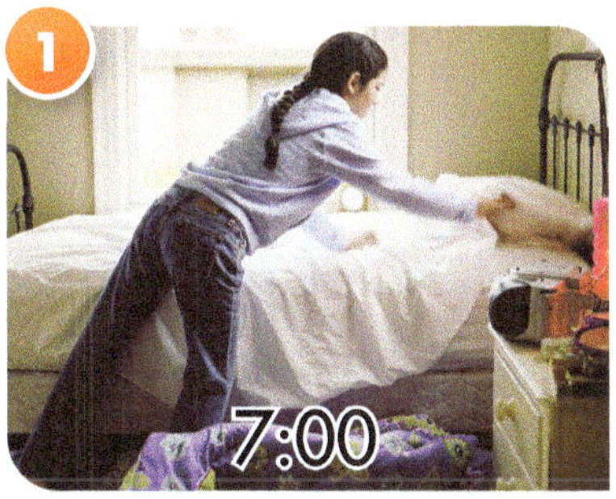

1. I *don't* make the bed at eight o'clock.
   I *make the bed at seven o'clock*.
2. Tony *doesn't* eat lunch at one o'clock.
   He *eats lunch at* ______________.
3. They ________ go to the park at ten o'clock.
   They ____________________________.
4. We ________ eat dinner at five o'clock.
   We ____________________________.
5. The baby ________ take a bath at two o'clock.
   He ____________________________.
6. Sue ________ go to bed at twelve o'clock.
   She ____________________________.

Simple present, interrogative

FISH: **Do** you **eat** dinner at five o'clock?

BIRD: No, I eat dinner at four o'clock.

FISH: **What do** you **eat** for dinner?

BIRD: I eat fish.

FISH: Oh. I go home at three o'clock!

1 Look and write.

1. *Does* Leo *eat* dinner at eight o'clock? *Yes, he does*.
2. ______ Jack ______ soccer at four o'clock? *No,* ______.
3. ______ May and Grace ______ home at five o'clock? ______.
4. ______ Mom ______ her bike at nine o'clock? ______.

2 Circle, write, and draw.

1. ***Does*** / ***Do*** you eat breakfast at seven o'clock?

   ______________________.

2. What ***do*** / ***does*** you eat for breakfast?

   ______________________.

Simple present, *Who?* 25

1 Look and write.

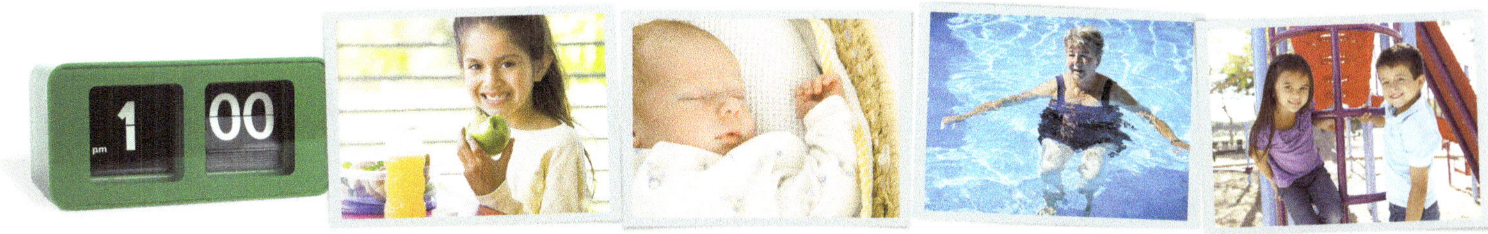

Kim | the baby | Grandma | Lucy and Bill

Ben | Ann | Grandpa | Jill

1. (*eat*) Who eats ______ lunch at one o'clock? ___Kim___
2. (*swim*) Who ______ at four o'clock? ______
3. (*sleep*) ______ at one o'clock? ______
4. (*play*) ______ on the playground at one o'clock? ______
5. (*eat*) ______ dinner at four o'clock? ______
6. (*sleep*) ______ at four o'clock? ______
7. (*play*) ______ on the playground at four o'clock? ______
8. (*swim*) ______ at one o'clock? ______

2 Write, look, and circle.

Dan
5:00 play soccer
7:00 eat dinner
8:00 watch TV
9:00 go to bed

Nick
5:00 play soccer
6:00 eat dinner
7:00 play piano
8:00 go to bed

1. *Dan / eat dinner*

   What time does Dan eat dinner ? **seven o'clock** (circled) / **six o'clock**

2. *Dan / watch TV*

   ______________________________? **eight o'clock / nine o'clock**

3. *Nick / play the piano*

   ______________________________? **eight o'clock / seven o'clock**

4. *they / play soccer*

   ______________________________? **five o'clock / six o'clock**

5. *Dan / go to bed*

   ______________________________? **eight o'clock / nine o'clock**

6. *Nick / eat dinner*

   ______________________________? **six o'clock / five o'clock**

3 Ask a friend. Then write.

What time do you...

eat lunch?

play?

go to bed?

Name: ____________________

____:00 ____________________

____:00 eat lunch

____:00 ____________________

4 Listen and number.

26

bedroom

living room

1

dining room

1. Where does Anna read?
2. Where does Anna's mom make dinner?
3. Where does Anna's family eat?
4. Where do they watch TV after dinner?

kitchen

5 Read and write.

Bill
9:00 school
12:00 lunch
3:00 the park
5:00 go home

1. Where does Bill go at nine o'clock?
   He goes to school at nine o'clock.
2. Who eats lunch at twelve o'clock?
   ____________________.
3. What time does Bill go to the park?
   ____________________.
4. What does Bill do at five o'clock?
   ____________________.

1 Listen and write. 27

ALEX: What do you do in the ____*morning*____?

TOM: I make __________. I eat __________.

ALEX: So do I! What do you do in the __________?

TOM: I play __________.

ALEX: Oh, I don't play __________.

I have too much __________!

TOM: I do my __________

at __________.

What do you do at

__________?

ALEX: I __________!

2 Read the dialogue with a friend.

3 Talk with a friend. Then write.

A: What do you do in the morning?

B: I __________. I __________.

A: What do you do in the afternoon?

B: I __________.

A: I don't __________. I __________.

B: What do you do at night?

A: I __________.

Let's sing!

1 Listen, read, and mark (✓ or ✗). 28

Tell Me About Bears

1. Where do bears live,
Can you tell me please?
They live in the mountains
And hide among the trees.

2. What do bears eat,
Can you tell me, please?
They eat lots of honey
They steal from the bees.

3. When do bears sleep,
Can you tell me, please?
They sleep all winter
In caves under leaves.

✗

All bears eat fish.

Bears look for honey.

Bears sleep in caves all winter.

Bears live among the trees.

Grammar summary

Unit 1

Possessive adjectives

My lunch box is small.	**Our** father is sad.
Your bag is big.	**Your** book is purple.
His cat is happy. **Her** dog is tall. **Its** house is blue.	**Their** snake is long.

Prepositions

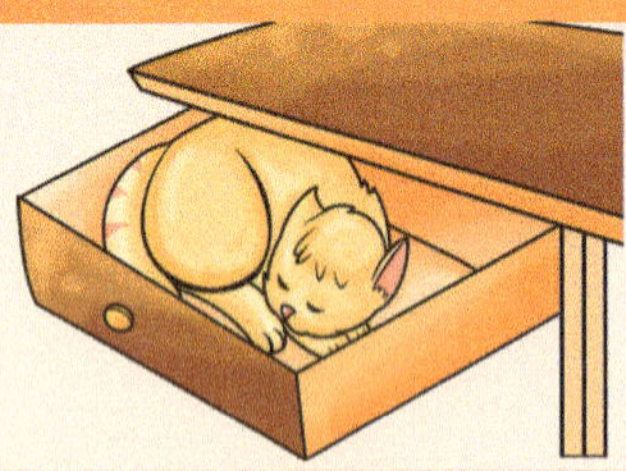		
in	on	under

Where...?

Where is my book?	It's under the bed.
Where are your dogs?	They're in the house.

Unit 2

Prepositions

in front of	behind	next to	between

Countable nouns with *some, any*

There are some gardens.	There aren't any flowers.

Are there any trees? Yes, there are. / No, there aren't.

How many...?

How many books are there? How many beds are in the kitchen?	There are ten books. There aren't any beds.

Unit 3

Plural nouns, regular

banana → bananas   tomato → tomatoes

Plural nouns, irregular

child → children		man → men
fish → fish		mouse → mice
foot → feet		woman → women

Demonstrative pronouns

This is an apple.	That is an orange.	These are apples.	Those are oranges.

Is this / that an apple?
Yes, it is. / No, it isn't.

Are these / those apples?
Yes, they are. / No, they aren't.

Unit 4

Possessive pronouns

The lunch box is **mine**.	The fish are **ours**.
This shirt is **yours**.	These socks are **yours**.
The baseball is **his**. The camera is **hers**.	That house is **theirs**.

Present continuous, affirmative

I	am	(I'm)	
You	are	(You're)	
He She It	is	(He's) (She's) (It's)	jumping. swimming. watching TV. wearing a new dress.
We You They	are	(We're) (You're) (They're)	

Present continuous, negative

I	am	not	(I'm not)	eating watermelon. sleeping. taking a picture. wearing new shoes.
You	are		(You aren't)	
He She It	is		(He isn't) (She isn't) (It isn't)	
We You They	are		(We aren't) (You aren't) (They aren't)	

Present continuous, interrogative

Am	I	running? talking? playing the piano? wearing T-shirts?	Yes, you are. / No, you're not.
Are	you		Yes, I am. / No, I'm not.
Is	he she it		Yes, he is. / No, he isn't. Yes, she is. / No, she isn't. Yes, it is. / No, it isn't.
Are	we you they		Yes, you are. / No, you aren't. Yes, we are. / No, we aren't. Yes, they are. / No, they aren't.

What are you doing?

What	am	I	doing?	You're	singing. drinking juice. playing baseball. painting a new picture.
	are	you		I'm	
	is	he she it		He's She's It's	
	are	we you they		We're You're They're	

Unit 5

Present continuous with adjectives	
You're wearing a **beautiful** dress!	Yes, but I'm wearing **ugly** shoes.

Countable nouns	
an apple	a carrot
a banana	an orange

Uncountable nouns	
cake	chocolate
cheese	meat

Uncountable nouns with *some, any*	
There is some milk.	There isn't any chicken.
Is there any ice cream? Yes, there is. / No, there isn't.	

Uncountable nouns with *a little, a lot*

There is a little juice.

There is a lot of juice.

Unit 6

***Can* for ability, affirmative**		
I	can	walk.
You		drive a car.
He She It		pick up the toys.
We You They		draw a picture.

***Can* for ability, negative**		
I	can't	swim.
You		fly a plane.
He She It		catch the ball.
We You They		ride a motorcycle.

Can for ability, interrogative

Can	I	spell? drive a car? throw a ball? play soccer?	Yes, you can. / No, you can't.
	you		Yes, I can. / No, I can't.
	he she it		Yes, he can. / No, he can't. Yes, she can. / No, she can't. Yes, it can. / No, it can't.
	we you they		Yes, you can. / No, you can't. Yes, we can. / No, we can't. Yes, they can. / No, they can't.

Commands

Pick up your toys. Hit the ball. Spell a word. Give me some juice, please.	Don't talk. Don't jump on the bed. Don't put your feet on the table. Don't run in the house, please.

Unit 7

Like, affirmative

I You	like	animals. lemonade. sleeping. jumping on the bed.
He She It	likes	
We You They	like	

Like, negative

I You	don't	like	milk. peas. riding bikes. swimming.
He She It	doesn't		
We You They	don't		

Like, interrogative				
Do	I	like	spiders? motorcycles? reading? playing games?	Yes, you do. / No, you don't.
	you			Yes, I do. / No, I don't.
Does	he she it			Yes, he does. / No, he doesn't. Yes, she does. / No, she doesn't. Yes, it does. / No, it doesn't.
Do	we you they			Yes, you do. / No, you don't. Yes, we do. / No, we don't. Yes, they do. / No, they don't.

What do you like?						
What	do	I you	like?	I You	like	flowers. yellow pears. fishing. making cookies.
	does	he she it		He She It	likes	
	do	we you they		We You They	like	

Which... do you like?							
Which	animal food hobby sport	do	I you	like?	I You	like	elephants. burgers. playing the guitar. tennis.
		does	he she it		He She It	likes	
		do	we you they		We You They	like	

Telling time

What time is it? It's three o'clock.	What time is it? It's seven o'clock.	What time is it? It's twelve o'clock.

Simple present, affirmative

I You	eat breakfast in the morning.
He She It	eats lunch in the afternoon.
We You They	eat dinner in the evening.

Simple present, negative

I You	don't	eat eggs in the morning. play soccer at three o'clock. go to the playground at night.
He She It	doesn't	
We You They	don't	

Simple present, interrogative			
Do	I	wake up at six o'clock? go to school at eight? eat dinner at seven o'clock? go to bed at ten o'clock?	Yes, you do. / No, you don't.
	you		Yes, I do. / No, I don't.
Does	he she it		Yes, he does. / No, he doesn't. Yes, she does. / No, she doesn't. Yes, it does. / No, it doesn't.
Do	we you they		Yes, you do. / No, you don't. Yes, we do. / No, we don't. Yes, they do. / No, they don't.

Who...?			
Who	wakes up at six o'clock? goes to the park? plays tennis at three o'clock? washes the dishes?	I You	do.
		He She It	does.
		We You They	do.

Audio script

Unit 1

Track 1
BOY 1: Is the elephant in the zoo?
BOY 2: No, it isn't. It's in the street!

Track 2
FATHER: Where are the pears?
GIRL: They're under here. Here you are.
FATHER: Thank you!
GIRL: Where is the ice cream?
FATHER: It's in here. Here you are.
GIRL: Thank you!

Track 3
At School
(See page 13.)

Unit 2

Track 4
BOY: I'm behind you! What's happening? What's it doing? Can you look?
GIRL: No! I can't look! My hands are in front of my eyes!
GIRL AND BOY: Eek!

Track 5
1. DAD: The baby is sleepy!
MOM: Well, he can't sleep in the kitchen! There aren't any beds!
VOICE: How many beds are in the kitchen?

2. VOICEOVER: Today, on "Animals All Around Us:" Cats in our homes! But where are they? Look, there's one! It's hiding behind the table!
VOICE: How many cats are behind the table?

3. VOICEOVER: Brad plays the piano. May sings. Daisy plays the guitar. May and Daisy are always in front of the piano. Then everyone can see them.
VOICE: How many people are in front of the piano?

4. GARDEN SHOW HOST: My favorite colors are yellow and white. So in my garden, there are only two colors of flowers: yellow and white!
VOICE: How many colors are in the garden?

5. SPORTS ANNOUNCER: The Harlem Globetrotters are amazing! Some of them are here now! You can see five of them behind their basketballs! They're wearing red uniforms.
VOICE: How many Harlem Globetrotters are behind the basketballs?

Track 6
WOMAN: Tom, what would you like for a snack?
BOY: I would like some grapes.
WOMAN: I'm sorry! There aren't any grapes. But there are some apples. Would you like an apple?
BOY: No, thank you. I'd like a pear.
WOMAN: Here you are.
BOY: Thank you!

Track 7
What Is It?
(See page 23.)

Unit 3

Track 8

BOY: Hey, Sue! Are these lizards? They're really big.
GIRL: No, Bob! Those aren't lizards. Those are crocodiles!
BOY: Aaaaaah!

Track 9

ALEX: I like frogs. Do you like frogs, too?
BILL: Yes, I do. And I love mice!
SUE: Me too! Do you like lizards?
BILL: I love lizards!
ALEX: So do I!

Track 10

We're Different

He has brown eyes,
Her hair is blond.
She has green eyes,
His legs are long.

We're different,
We're not the same.
We all like to play this game.

She has black hair,
And he's short.
We're great friends,
I like them all.

We're different,
We're not the same.
We all like to play this game,
To play this game,
To play this game.

Unit 4

Track 11

BOY: Oh, look! Sam is watching TV.
GIRL: Funny dog. He's watching the ball. The ball is bouncing away. Uh, oh! No, Sam!

Track 12

TONY: Hi! I'm Tony. I have a white baseball. I have a small helicopter. I have a yellow clock.
LUCY: I'm his sister. My name is Lucy. I have a black camera. I have a purple basketball. I have a short robot.
TONY: Our family has a cat.
LUCY: Our cat is orange.
TONY: We have a big TV.
LUCY: And we have a small radio.
TONY: And we both have…
TONY AND LUCY: …blue bikes!

Track 13

GRACE: What do you like to do?
TOM: I like walking the dog.
GRACE: So do I. Do you like fishing?
TOM: Yes, I do. Fishing is fun.
GRACE: Do you like cleaning?
TOM: No, I don't!
GRACE: I don't, either!

Track 14

What Time Is it?

What time is it?
It's six o'clock.
Is Hannah in the kitchen?
Yes, she is. Yes, she is.
What's she doing in the kitchen?
She's making dinner for all of us.

What time is it?
It's eight o'clock.
Is Raymond in the bathroom?
Yes, he is. Yes, he is.
What's he doing in the bathroom?
He's taking a shower and singing a song.

What time is it?
It's nine o'clock.
Is Calvin in the bedroom?
Yes, he is. Yes, he is.
What's he doing in the bedroom?
He's wearing pajamas and reading a book.

Unit 5

Track 15

MOTHER: Are you wearing dirty shoes? Are you eating chocolate?
SON: I'm cleaning my room, Mom!
MOTHER: Oh, okay!

Track 16

DAD: Would you like some cereal?
SARA: Yes, please. I'd like a little cereal.
DAD: And would you like an apple?
SARA: Yes, please, I'd like one.
DAD: Would you like any water?
SARA: No, thank you. But I'd like some juice.

Track 17

A Costume Party

(See page 53.)

Unit 6

Track 18

MOTHER SNAKE: We can't pick up shellsssss.
CHILDREN SNAKES: Awwww. We can't sssssswim.
FATHER SNAKE: But we can ride in a boat!

Track 19

1. ANNOUNCER: This is Sam.
GIRL: Hi, Sam. What can you do?
SAM: I can pick up three watermelons!
ANNOUNCER AND GIRL: Cool!

2. BOY: Hi, Ann. Hi, Grace. What can you do?
ANN: We can walk a lot of dogs.
BOY: How many dogs can you walk?
GRACE: We can walk 12 dogs!
BOY: Wow!

3. BOY: Hi, Mr. Bill. How many children can you see in your bus?
MR. BILL: There are a lot of children. I can see seventeen!

4. BOY: Hi, monkeys. How many bananas can you eat?
BOY: They can eat 14 bananas! Wow!

5. BOY: Jill! Don't take a photo of me!
JILL: I can take 20 photos if I want to!
BOY: Good-bye!

6. BOY: Hi, Mom. How many cakes can you make?
BOY'S MOM: Oh, I can only make one cake! But it's your favorite—chocolate! Look.

Track 20

GIRL: Let's make a robot. Find a box.
BOY: Okay. What now?
GIRL: Cut some circles for eyes. Draw a mouth.
BOY: Okay. What's next?
GIRL: Put the box on your head.
BOY: Look! I'm a robot!

Track 21

Pets

Rabbits can jump.
Cats can run.
Spiders can climb
Up to the sun!

Chorus:
They're good,
They're bad,
They're happy,
They're sad!

Fish can swim.
Dogs can run.
Parrots can fly
Up to the sun!

(Chorus)

Unit 7

Track 22

BOY: Here are some flowers, Miss May.
TEACHER: Thank you! I like flowers. What do you like, Bill?
BOY: I like spiders! And look—there's one, right there!
TEACHER: Eeek!

Track 23

BOY 1: Would you like to ride bikes?
BOY 2: No, thanks. I don't like riding bikes. I like fishing.
BOY 1: Sorry, I don't like fishing.
BOY 2: Would you like to play soccer?
BOY 1: Yes! Do you have a ball?
BOY 2: No.

Track 24
I Like Food
(See page 73.)

Unit 8

Track 25

GRANDMOTHER: Who plays tennis at three o'clock?
BOYS: We do, Grandmother!
GRANDMOTHER: Who goes to the park at four o'clock?
Girl: I do, Grandmother!
GRANDMOTHER: Who cleans the kitchen at five o'clock?
BOYS: She does!
GIRL: They do!

Track 26

1. GIRL: I'm Anna. At four o'clock, I read in the dining room.
My brother Sam listens to the radio in his bedroom.
2. GIRL: At five o'clock, Sam plays the guitar in the living room.
Mom makes dinner in the kitchen.
3. GIRL: At six o'clock, we eat dinner in the living room.
4. GIRL: At seven o'clock, we all watch TV in my bedroom!

Track 27

ALEX: What do you do in the morning?
TOM: I make the bed. I eat breakfast.
ALEX: So do I! What do you do in the afternoon?
TOM: I play baseball.
ALEX: Oh, I don't play baseball. I have too much homework!
TOM: I do my homework at night. What do you do at night?
ALEX: I sleep!

Track 28
Tell Me About Bears
(See page 83.)

Vocabulary

afternoon 74
alphabet 24
animals 64
baby 64
baseball 24
basketball 34
bath 74
bathroom 14
beach 54
beautiful 44
bed 74
bedroom 14
behind 14
between 14
bird 24
boat 54
body 24
bookstore 4
bounce 34
box 4
breakfast 74
burger 64
bus 54
cake 44
camera 34
child 24
children 24
chocolate 44
clean (*adj*) 44
clean (*v*) 34
close 34
crocodile 24
cut 54
dining room 14
dinner 74
dirty 44
door 34
drive 54
duck 14
egg 64
evening 74
face 24
family 64
father 4
fish (*n*) 44
fish (*v*) 34
floor 54
food 44, 64
french fries 64
fries 64
frog 4
fruit 44
garden 14
give 54
go home 74
go to bed 74
go to school 74
go to sleep 74
go to the park 74
hair 24
hamburger 64
head 24
hit 34
hobby 64
hobbies 64
in 4
in front of 14
jacket 44
jeans 44
juice 44
kick 34
kitchen 14
legs 24
lemon 64
lemonade 64
letter 24
living room 14
lizard 24
lunch 74
make 54
make the bed 74
man 24
men 24
mango 64
meat 44
mirror 14
monkey 24
morning 74
mother 4
motorcycle 54
new 44
next to 14
night 74
old 44, 64
on 4
onion 64
open 34
orange
paint 4
park 4
peas 64
pick up 54
plane 54
play baseball 34
play tennis 34
playground 4
radio 14
rice 44
rooms 14
sand 54
sea 54
shell 54
sleep 74
spell 54
spider 64
sports 64
store
street 4
sun 54
tail 24
take a bath 74
television 14
toys 14
truck 4
TV 14
ugly 44
under 4
walk 34
watch 34
watermelon 44
woman 24
women 24
young 64
zoo 4